☞ **W9-AQZ-965**

3 9082 02044153 4

Copy 6

J
688.763 Arnow, Jan, 1947-
A   Louisville Slugger : the making of a
         baseball bat / written and photographed
         by Jan Arnow. -- 1st ed. -- New York :
         Pantheon Books, c1984.
            39 p. : ill. ; 21 x 23 cm.

            SUMMARY: A photo essay describing how
         baseball bats are made for the Hille-
         rich & Bradsby Company in Louisville,
         Kentucy.

            ISBN 0-394-96297-4 (lib. bdg.) : 6.00

         1.Baseball bats.   72797   F85

                                        dc19
                                                84-7049
 CATALOG CARD CORPORATION OF AMERICA®   AACR2   MARC AC 3

LOUISVILLE SLUGGER

THE MAKING OF A BASEBALL BAT

WRITTEN AND PHOTOGRAPHED BY

JAN ARNOW

PANTHEON BOOKS

NEW YORK

For Sam, Chloe, and Abraham, with love.

Enthusiastic thanks to Jack and Irvin H. Norton
and all of the employees at Larimer and Norton;
Bill Williams, Paul Galens, and all of the bat makers
at Hillerich & Bradsby's Slugger Park;
the Louisville Redbirds; the *Courier-Journal;* all of my
friends at the University of Louisville Photographic Archives;
my friend Pat Ross, who brought me into the world of
children's books; and my editor, Dinah Stevenson,
whose guidance has been and continues to be invaluable.

Endpaper photograph and pages 3, 36, 37, 38, 39 reprinted
with permission from *The Courier-Journal* and *The Louisville
Times.* Pages 22 and 27: Hillerich & Bradsby Co. Pages 4
and 35: Royal Collection, Photographic Archives,
University of Louisville.

Library of Congress Cataloging in Publication Data
Arnow, Jan, 1947–   Louisville Slugger.
Summary: A photo essay describing how
baseball bats are made for Hillerich & Bradsby Company
in Louisville, Kentucky.
1. Baseball bats—Juvenile literature. [1. Baseball
bats] I. Title.
GV867.5.A76 1984   688.7′6357   84-7049
ISBN 0-394-86297-X   ISBN 0-394-96297-4 (lib. bdg.)

BASEBALL has been our favorite warm-weather sport for more than a century. From early spring until fall, people of every age gather to watch their favorite teams play or to play baseball themselves. At the end of the season the whole country tunes in to the World Series to see who will be our champion team for the year. And the names of famous baseball players like Babe Ruth, Hank Aaron, and Pete Rose are among the names we know best.

But who do you think is the oldest star in baseball? It's not a famous player or manager or a well-known team. It's the baseball bat. Without the bat, baseball would be nothing more than a game of catch.

In the early days of baseball, players bought bats from local woodturners or made their own. The first known custom-made baseball bat was made in 1884 by John "Bud" Hillerich, a young apprentice in his father's wood-turning shop in Louisville, Kentucky. On a warm spring day that year, he sneaked off from his job to watch the Louisville Eclipse team play a few innings. During that game, Pete "Old Gladiator" Browning, the Eclipses' best hitter, broke his bat. After the game young Hillerich offered to make him a new one. Browning agreed and went with Hillerich to his dad's shop, where they selected a sturdy piece of white-ash timber. Hillerich put the piece of wood on a lathe and gradually shaped it into a bat, with Browning testing it every few turns until it was just right.

Photographed in the late 1880s, Bud Hillerich is in the doorway holding a bat; his father is the second man from the left.

In the next day's game Browning went three for three and gave the credit for his three long hits to his new bat. After that game the rest of the Eclipse team showed up at the Hillerich shop and demanded bats for themselves. So began the bat business for J. F. Hillerich and his son Bud. And for one hundred years the family business—now called Hillerich & Bradsby—has been making Louisville Slugger professional baseball bats the same way.

The making of Louisville Slugger baseball bats begins in a forest in Pennsylvania. Each weekday morning a forester "cruises the timber" in search of suitable ash trees. Only ash wood has the strength, flexibility, and light weight that are needed for a bat that will drive the baseball over the fence. It takes forty to sixty years to grow an ash tree that is fourteen to sixteen inches in diameter at chest height, the right size for use in making baseball bats. When the forester finds a tall, straight ash tree that size, he marks it with spray paint to identify it for the log cutter.

The log cutter studies the marked tree carefully to determine which way it should fall so that it won't damage other trees on the way down. He wants it to land in a place that will be easy to get to with his tractor, so he can bring it out later.

He cuts out a wedge from the base of the tree with his chain saw. The opening of the wedge points in the direction that the tree will fall. Next he cuts into the opposite side of the base and puts a small metal wedge into the cut. This will prevent the tree from falling over backward.

Starting from the original wedge cut, he saws through the base. Suddenly there is a loud CRACK! The tree falls forward and hits the forest floor with a great thud, right where he wanted it to land.

The log cutter cuts off the top of the tree, which will be left in the forest for people who collect firewood. He then places a metal cable choker around the base of the tree and reels in the cable with a winch that is attached to his tractor. He drags the log out of the heart of the forest to a cleared area called a log landing.

There he saws the log into ten- to sixteen-foot lengths. He uses the front of his tractor to push the short logs into a pile, where they will wait to be picked up and taken to the mill.

When the log landing is full, a log truck makes its way into the forest. The driver picks the logs off the pile with the truck's powerful clam lifter and drops them onto the bed of the truck. He chains the load in place and drives out of the forest to the lumber mill.

At the millyard the logs are unchained.

As the clam lifter places the logs on the ground, a man called a scaler climbs up the logs and measures, or scales, each one.

The scaler then tallies up the measurements and pays the driver for hauling the logs. This truck unloaded over three thousand board feet of lumber: a board foot is twelve inches long by twelve inches wide by one inch thick.

A forklift driver brings the logs to the skidway, where they are placed on chains that roll them down to a hydraulic chain saw. They are cut into pieces that average forty inches long.

An important part of the chain saw operator's job is rejecting the wood that is not good enough to become Louisville Slugger bats. If a log is flawed by knots or the grain isn't straight, he sets it aside, and it is later sold for other uses. Only half of the wood that is cut in the forest ends up as baseball bats.

The choicest wood is now turned into billets, the smooth, rounded forms from which the bats will be made. There are several ways to do this, but most commonly the forty-inch log is rolled down to a hydraulic wedge that easily divides it into six to eight pieces called splits.

From here the splits go to a lathe that automatically turns each one, shaving off all the rough edges.

At the end of the day the billets are divided into two groups. Those with the straightest grain will become professional bats, which are made by hand. The factory turns out some twelve thousand professional bats a year—and about 1 million machine-made nonprofessional bats.

The billets are then stacked and strapped into six-sided bundles, and the ends are painted with a preservative to protect them during the long trip to Slugger Park.

Early in the morning about once a week, a truck arrives at Slugger Park in Jeffersonville, Indiana, just across the Ohio River from Louisville, Kentucky, carrying the billets from the sawmills in Pennsylvania.

Because there is still a lot of moisture in the wood, the billets must go through a drying-out process called seasoning. The stacks of billets are left in the factory yard from six months to two years to let the water evaporate from them. Sometimes there are more than a million pieces of wood stacked in the yard.

When they are finally dry, the billets are again inspected for quality and weighed.

Each billet is then placed on an automatic lathe, where it is roughly shaped so that it begins to look like a baseball bat.

These bat forms are sanded, checked for quality yet again, and sorted into stacks by weight before going through the final steps in their journey from forest to playing field.

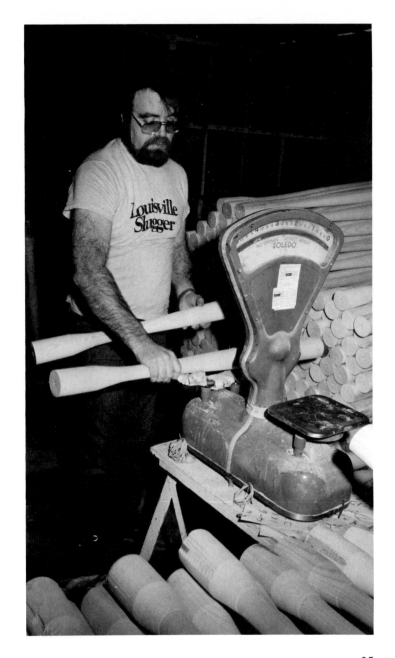

The mail arrives at the offices of Hillerich & Bradsby in Louisville, Kentucky, bringing orders for bats from major and minor league baseball teams all over the country. The orders are taken to the factory at Slugger Park, where microfilm files contain complete records of the models every player uses. The average player uses more than seventy bats every season.

A player might order a dozen of the model that Johnny Bench used. Or he will want six of Hank Aaron's model and six of Ted Williams's model. Or, most likely, he will want his own model, one of the thousands that are kept in the huge archive room at Slugger Park.

The model is retrieved from the archive room, where bins are filled from floor to ceiling with bats of the famous and not-so-famous in baseball history. The bats are all different weights and all different sizes, ranging in length from 30½ inches (Willie Keeler's bat) to 36 inches (Babe Ruth's bat). The rulebook states only that the length of a professional bat cannot exceed 42 inches, nor the diameter of the barrel exceed 2¾ inches, so the variety is tremendous.

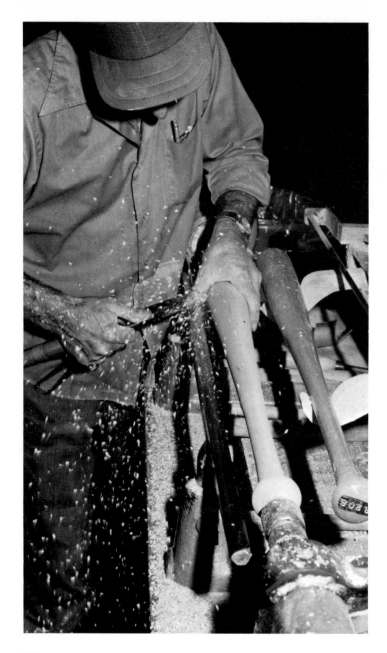

The model bat is given to one of the people in the factory who are specially trained to make professional bats.

The bat turner begins by taking a sanded bat form from the stack that most closely approximates the model bat in weight and length and placing it on a lathe. The model bat goes on a rack just above and behind it.

Then he turns the unfinished wood form on the lathe, gradually shaving and sanding it into just the bat the player requires, exactly the same way Bud Hillerich first did one hundred years ago.

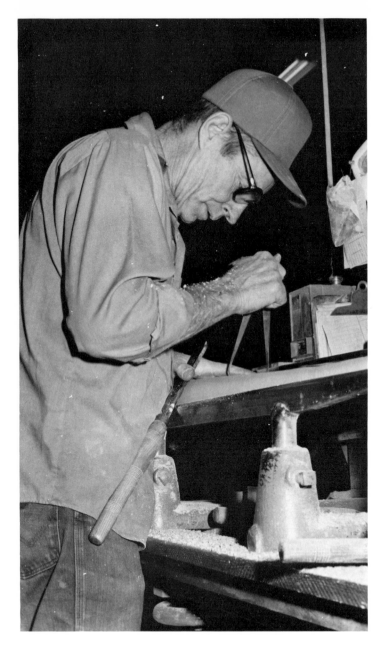

With calipers, the bat turner frequently checks the measurements of the new bat against the model, every inch along the handle and every 1½ to 2 inches along the barrel, and weighs it carefully at every stage until it matches the model exactly.

When the bat meets the player's exact specifications, it is burn branded with the Louisville Slugger trademark and the player's signature.

The trademark is put about a quarter turn from the "sweet spot," the place on the barrel that should make contact with the ball. When the ball hits this spot, the force of the impact is distributed evenly throughout the bat, and the batter will never feel a sting or shock from vibration. This is why a player is never supposed to hit the ball with the trademark side of the bat.

After the bat is branded, the knobs at the ends—by which the bat was held in the various machines—are cut off and sanded down. The bat is stained a darker color, if the player requires it, and given a coat of varnish.

The finished bats are packed and shipped to the team.

Baseball players have always been very particular about how their bats are made and treated. Frank Frisch hung his Louisville Sluggers in a barn during the off-season to cure them like sausages. When Ted Williams was on a hitting streak, he gave his bats alcohol baths to cool them off. Williams used to spend hours at the factory looking for billets with narrow growth rings, believing that they made the best hitters.

Babe Ruth

Babe Ruth liked little pin knots in the barrels of his bats. The billets used for Hugh Duffy's bats had to ring a certain way when they were bounced on a concrete floor or he wouldn't accept them. Ty Cobb used the same bat model for over twenty-five years. But some players change the size and weight of their bat as often as their mood changes.

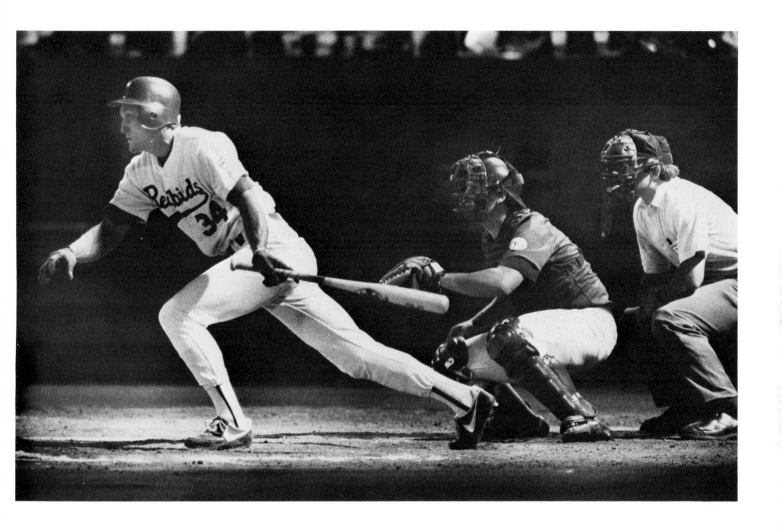

Many players nowadays further personalize their bats when they receive them from the factory. A player may stain the handle of a new bat with pine tar or wrap it to increase the grip, but only up to eighteen inches from the knob of the bat, which is all the rulebook allows. Some players oil their bats, and others even rub tobacco juice into theirs.

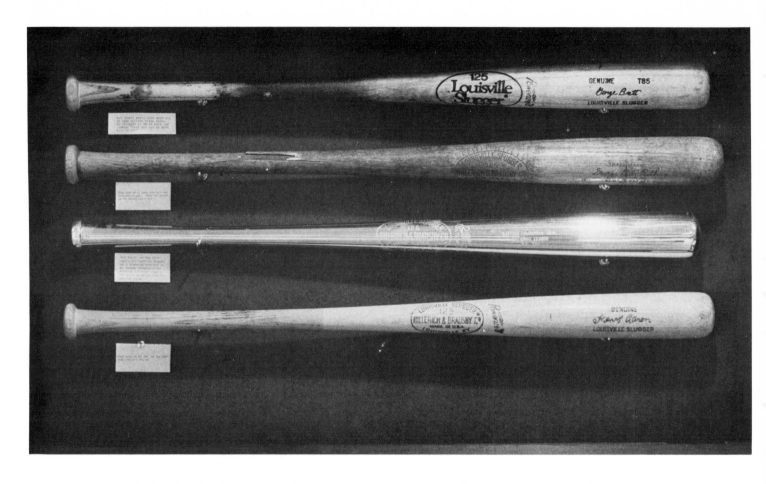

Today, Louisville Slugger bats are used by every single major and minor league baseball team in the United States. They are made all year round in the busy 6½-acre factory at Slugger Park, just outside of Louisville, Kentucky. Visitors to the factory can watch the step-by-step bat-making process and have a look at Hillerich & Bradsby's most famous bats: Babe Ruth's, with a notch for every home run he made with it; the bat Hank Aaron used to hit seven hundred home runs; a sterling silver bat, and many more. Sometimes an entire ball team will stop by the factory on their way back from spring training.

The next time you go to the ball park to see your favorite team play, or when you see a ball game on television, or when you just get together with some friends to hit a few, you'll recognize the real star of the game—the Louisville Slugger baseball bat!

Jan Arnow has a B.F.A. degree from the School of the Art Institute, Chicago. She has founded, owned, and managed a variety of businesses; designed and taught courses and workshops in serigraphy, alternative photographic processes, textile design, visual communications, the business of art, and hand bookbinding; and served as executive director of the Art Center Association in Louisville, Kentucky. Ms. Arnow's photographs and prints, hand-bound books, and photographic quilts have been widely exhibited and have won numerous awards. The author of *Lightworks: A Handbook of Photographic Alternatives*, Ms. Arnow lives in Louisville with her husband and three small children. In her spare time, she conducts workshops and gives lectures, does consulting work, and still finds time for writing and photography.